THE BUSINESS OF WRITING

WRITING LESSONS FROM THE FRONT, BOOK 14

ANGELA HUNT

Hunt Haven

Other Lessons in the **Writing Lessons from the Front**

1. The Plot Skeleton
2. Creating Extraordinary Characters
3. Point of View
4. Track Down the Weasel Words
5. Evoking Emotion
6. Plans and Processes to Get Your Book Written
7. Tension on the Line
8. Writing Historical Fiction
9. The Fiction Writer's Book of Checklists
10. Writing the Picture Book
11. The First Fifty Pages of your Novel
12. The Art of Revision
13. Writing Dialogue
14. The Business of Writing

A Christian Writer's Possibly Useful Ruminations on a Life in Pages,
supplemental volume

Visit Angela Hunt's website at www.angelahuntbooks.com.
The Business of Writing, Copyright 2024, Angela Hunt.
Published by Hunt Haven Press. All rights reserved. Do not reproduce or
share these pages without permission from the publisher.
ISBN paper: 978-1961394834
ISBN ebook: 978-1961394841

INTRODUCTION

I never dreamed of being a writer. Never even considered it, though I did try to pen a novel in the fifth grade. I was a musician, you see, so I majored in music and even took a year out to travel and sing with a ten-member ensemble.

But during that traveling and singing, my group just happened to get stuck overnight in a Colorado blizzard. We spent four days and nights with a family of five who took us in and let us enact an episode of *Survivor*, except in a blizzard. With very little food, we resorted to making pancakes in the fireplace with Bisquick and melted snow. We had no electricity and no running water, but we were young and energetic and I remember thinking it was the adventure of a lifetime. (I had never seen snow until a few months before.) During our snowbound adventure, we wrote in our journals, and when we were finally back on the road, we shared our journals with our director, who hadn't been with us.

About a month later, we were on another all-night drive. I was navigating for our director, Derric Johnson, who was driving. Two other group members were dozing in the back seat.

Pastor Derric—that's what we called him, because that's what he was to us—asked what I wanted to do when I came off the road. "I guess I'll go back to college," I said. "I'll finish my music degree and teach or something . . ."

Pastor Derric took his eyes off the road long enough to smile at me. "I read your journal," he said, "And you have a way with words. You ought to consider writing."

And because I believe that God often speaks through the voices of our spiritual authorities, I said, "Okay."

I went back to college on a music scholarship, but I changed my major to English. Liberty Baptist College was a fledgling school in those days, but they had an English major. I signed up for classes that included modern grammar, Chaucer, Shakespeare, and seventeenth century poetry.

I graduated with honors in English on Monday, May 12th, and got married on Tuesday, May 13th. And though I had absolutely no idea what I'd do with a music minor and an English major, I knew I'd need to help pay the family bills. I had married a youth pastor, and the youth pastor always seems to be fairly far down the salary totem pole.

The Lord works in mysterious ways. During my senior year, during which I only took a couple of classes, the local Christian school dismissed a high school English teacher after only a couple of weeks. They were desperate for a teacher, and I was desperate for a full-time job, so I found myself teaching high school juniors and seniors about American and British Literature. I loved teaching—still do —but since I'd had no education classes, I was not well-equipped to deal with kids—many of whom were determined to give me a hard time.

The next year I worked for a church, writing curriculum. The next year I worked as a secretary for a national organization's communications director. Finally, I decided that if I was ever going to be a writer, I might as well step out and be one.

But how does one get started? *Any way you can.*

I handed in my resignation and had business cards printed up: **Angela Hunt, freelance writer.** I sent them to all the advertising agencies in town, figuring that they might need freelance writers.

Lo and behold, one of them called me. The man said to come to his office and bring my portfolio, so I went to the office supply store and wandered the aisles until I found something that said *portfolio*. It was empty, of course, so I filled it with plastic page protectors. And then, still aware that it was painfully lacking, I printed out a copy of my resume that listed my former jobs: Singer. Teacher, Administrative Assistant.

But before the interview, I went to the library and picked up a book called *Dress for Success*. So you can bet I was dressed appropriately—a nice red dress, white jacket, a red flower on the lapel.

I went downtown, shook the man's hand, and took the seat he offered. "Let me see your portfolio," he said, so I handed it to him.

He opened it and looked at me. "It's empty."

"I know," I said, blushing. "I'm new."

The man smiled, leaned back in his chair, and took a deep breath. "Okay," he said, pulling a catalog from his desk. "We produce a catalog for—" and he named a company that made fiberglass mailboxes. "Here's last year's catalog. Here's a sheet featuring their new products. Write up some copy for these new products and send me an invoice."

"Okay, I will."

Honestly, the job was pretty much a no-brainer, but I examined the previous year's catalog, wrote similar descriptions of the new mailboxes, and almost felt guilty when I filled out an invoice and charged the man twenty dollars for an hour of work.

When he handed me a check, I knew I could be a professional writer.

So can you.

———

I don't remember much about my college classes, but I do remember being handed a brochure called "English as the Pre-Professional Major." The gist of the piece was that a student who could write well could excel in jobs that require clarity of thought and an ability to express those thoughts.

I found myself agreeing with the principle. I've always loved reading because it is through absorbing words that we equip ourselves to contemplate and express new thoughts. How can you express a profound idea if you don't have the right words?

The writing life is about feeling—there is an undeniable emotional component—but it's far more important that the writer be direct and succinct. A writer must understand the words and the emotional component of those words. The difference between *notorious* and *famous*. The difference between *requesting* something and *demanding* it.

If you are interested in earning a living through writing, I suggest you read voraciously. Parents of middle and high school students are always asking me how to encourage their young writers. I suspect they want me to tell their kids how to self-publish, but the best thing a young writer can do is *read*. Just because someone *can* self-publish doesn't meant mean they *should*, especially when they haven't gained enough experience to publish with excellence.

Just because I can carve a turkey doesn't mean I can perform brain surgery. Just because you wrote wonderful college essays doesn't meant mean you know how to write professionally. Because few people take professional writing classes in college, you're going to learn by *doing*. By reading books on writing craft. By going to conferences. And by experiencing rejection.

Our English teachers applauded when we pulled out our thesauruses and piled on the adjectives and adverbs in our prose, but you can't do that in professional writing. Professional writing is about communicating as much as possible in as few words as possible.

Becoming a professional writer isn't easy, but you can do it if you're willing to learn. You will never learn everything, and even if you could, writing styles will change and you'll learn how to change with them.

I've written a series about the craft of writing—brief, pointed lessons about the techniques you'll need to write well. I've also established a newsletter for professional writers.

But this writing lesson is about the *business* side of writing—all the things you have to learn in order to establish and run a writing business—all the things they don't teach in creative writing classes.

We're going to talk about submissions, writing for different markets, when and how to find an agent, how to approach a publisher, and if you should incorporate your business. We'll talk about how much money writers make, and how much you should charge if you hang out a shingle to write for those who are eager to self-publish their life stories. We'll talk about ghostwriting and collaborations and if they're a perfect fit for you. We'll even talk about taxes and tax deductions.

So settle back and get comfortable—away we go!

Chapter One

EMPLOYEE OR ENTREPRENEUR?

THE FIRST DECISION A WOULD-BE FULL-TIME WRITER HAS to make is this one: will you be a freelancer or will you work for a company? Do you want the reliability of a steady paycheck, or are you more thrilled by the thought of being an entrepreneur?

If you work for a magazine, newspaper, or other organization, you will be doing work for hire. Your employer will own all the rights to your work, but you will be compensated with a salary and employee benefits. You will write or edit for the company, and you will not be able to publish that work elsewhere.

The communications field has changed dramatically since the advent of the Internet, with many newspapers closing and more communication taking place on platforms like X and YouTube. Many magazines have gone completely digital. But the surviving companies and organizations still need writers.

Many people are happier living with the certainty of a steady paycheck and health insurance. If you don't like the idea of not knowing where your next check will come from, this route might be a good one for you.

If you're married and your spouse has a full-time job with benefits, however, freelance writing might be a better fit for you. You won't have to stress about not having enough money to pay the mortgage if your spouse's paycheck will cover the family bills as you're starting out.

Are people really hoping to hire freelance writers? Absolutely! Every week I am astounded to see how many companies look at my LinkedIn profile simply because I identify myself as a writer.

For instance, I have *just* received an email from LinkedIn, and it contains a list of companies currently looking for freelancers: Huckleberry Labs, the True Crime YouTube channel, Pocket FM, Anzir (they're looking for a freelance game writer), Mindrift, and Toloka. I have no idea who any of those groups are, but they're looking for writers.

Because freelance writers are self-employed, they can choose or reject jobs and can usually work from home, no matter where your home is. Freelancers are hired by companies that do both digital and print publications. They are often hired to train AI (artificial intelligence). An Internet search will reveal all kinds of companies looking for freelance writers. And don't forget the more traditional venues for freelancers: magazines (digital and print), newspapers, and book publishers.

When you sell your written material to a company, you will sell certain rights. Some companies will buy **all rights** to your piece and own it thereafter, possibly reprinting it in future volumes or gift books.

Some publications will buy **first rights** and have the right to run your piece before anyone else, leaving you with the option to sell the **second serial** or **reprint rights** to another publication. Companies typically pay more for all rights or first serial rights.

What will you be writing as a freelance writer? All kinds of things!

- Sports articles
- Interviews
- Puff pieces (interviews designed to make someone look good)
- Humor
- Columns (as a guest columnist or a regular contributor)
- Articles on business
- Articles on family issues
- Articles on pet health or training
- Nostalgia pieces
- Pieces about historical places, events, or people
- Articles about locals celebrating milestones
- Local interest

You may have a next door neighbor with a claim to fame, but no one knows about it. Your best friend may be an expert in some exotic field. You husband may hold a local school's record for the long jump, or your grandmother may have been a riveter during World War II. Has your child set a record for constant hiccuping? Has your dog been featured on *Live with Regis and Kelly*? (Mine was!)

Every person has a story, so don't be shy about getting to know people. You never know what fascinating story you may run across, and it may be perfect for a magazine or your local paper. Personality profiles are popular, and the personality doesn't have to be famous. Ordinary people can be fascinating if they've developed a special skill or have a fascinating history, so always be on the lookout for such stories.

Once you find something or someone to write about, you need a place to sell that story. You will find that in **Writer's Market**.

Chapter Two

WRITER'S MARKET

When I set out to become a writer, one of the first things I bought was a copy of the annual **Writer's Market**. I bought a new one every year and lined them up on my shelf like trophies. If the house had been on fire, I would have grabbed my wedding pictures and my battered **Writer's Market**.

Writer's Market has everything you didn't learn as an English major: Articles on how to write better queries. Sample query letters. A primer on publishers and their imprints. An article on how to find money to fund your learning curve. Articles on blogging, publishing, making money, how much to charge, and how to use social media to help reach your writing goals.

Within its pages you'll find a list of professional writer's organizations . . . a glossary . . . a book publishers subject index . . . a glossary of publishing terms . . . and a list of contests and awards for writers.

You'll find an encyclopedia of consumer magazines, complete with editor's names, how they prefer to receive submissions (mail or email), what they're looking for, and how much they pay. Ditto for trade journals for those who work in hotels, finance, entertainment, real estate, transportation, and more.

You'll find a complete list of literary agents and their contact info, and a *huge* listing of book publishers, with their addresses, email addresses, contact information, and what they're hoping to publish. You can learn if they pay an advance. How long they take to respond. And if they take simultaneous and/or unagented submissions.

I meet so many new writers who dream of writing a particular book . . . I want to tell them that if they'd put that book aside and start writing other things for a while, they'll probably learn—and *earn*—enough to make finishing that book a lot easier.

I have just opened the latest edition of **Writer's Market** to a random page and found the listing for *Boston Review* magazine.

The mailing address is listed, along with the editor's name and email, along with the magazine's website. They are 90 percent freelance written. They are "an online and print magazine of cultural and political analysis, reviews, fiction, and poetry." They accept queries by email and an online submission form. They accept simultaneous submissions. They respond to queries in about four months, and you can buy a sample copy or read the magazine for free online. Writing guidelines are available on the website. *Read the magazine* before querying, they advise, and I would second that motion. They buy 200 manuscripts per year and they need book excerpts, essays, exposes, general interest, historical, interview, reviews, and more.

Writers Market has hundreds of entries just like that one. And you can have all of them at your fingertips for a tax-deductible $20 (if you're a writer, it's a business expense). Here's a link, or search for it on Amazon.com.

There's also a Christian Writer's Market. My friend Steve Laube puts that reference together, and like its general market counterpart, the **Christian Writer's Market** has nearly 1,000 listings, including more than 200 book publishers, 130 periodical publishers, 45 specialty markets, 215 writer's conferences and writers groups around the world, 45 literary agencies, 240 freelance editors and designers, as well as dozens of legal and accounting services, speaking services, podcasts, courses, and contests.

The print version of **Christian Writer's Market** comes out every December, but the online version is updated throughout the year and is available for a reasonable price.

If you're serious about writing as a career, if you want your writing to pay some bills, you will appreciate the information in **Writer's Market**. Gather up some ideas and start submitting your articles. When you cash that first check, you'll be a professional writer. Do it often enough, and you could be a *full-time* professional writer.

Is it really that easy? You send an article to a magazine and wait for the checks to come in?

Not quite. You usually need an okay from the editor before you send in your article, and to get that permission, you need to write a letter or email. Not just any letter or email—a *well-crafted query,* which is almost as important as the article itself.

Chapter Three

THE QUERY LETTER

A QUERY LETTER IS A LETTER OR EMAIL DESIGNED TO quickly tell the editor who you are and what you are proposing to write. An editor will be impressed if you indicate—truthfully—that you are familiar with the magazine or publisher, so make sure you read some sample copies in print or online.

QUERY LETTER FOR A MAGAZINE

March 25, 2024
Mr. Joe Smith
Editor

Baxter Monthly
555 Union Street
Pottersville, NY 12345

Dear Mr. Smith:
    After reading the article on old trains in the June

edition of *Baxter Monthly*, I wondered if you are aware that a rare antique caboose currently resides in a Clearwater resident's front yard? The wooden caboose proudly bears the date March 21, 1925 and has been refurbished, but it rode the rails of the Atlantic Pacific railroad before it came to rest in my neighbor's yard. Would you be interested in a story about the artist whose passion for trains led him to find, purchase, and restore this amazing relic? I can send you an 800-word story within two weeks of receiving a green light from you.

I've published several articles in our local paper and am a frequent contributor to *Southern Living*. Thank you for your time and consideration. I look forward to hearing from you!

Sincerely,
Tanya Wilson
Tanya@gjskbll.com

LET'S ANALYZE THE LETTER.

First, the editor's address: even if this is emailed, I'd still copy the editor's address and include it in the email. Take pains to get the editor's name right and check your spelling. Be respectful of the editor's time by keeping your query short and to the point.

Next, notice that Tanya, our writer, has clearly indicated that she's read a copy of the magazine. She's not only read it, she remembered a particular article well enough to refer to it because it led to her idea—a story about a neighborhood caboose.

Tanya also points out that the article she's proposing isn't so much about the caboose, but about the artist who found, purchased, and restored the train. It's a personality profile about an artist who adores trains so much that he has one on his front lawn. Interesting!

Tanya gives the editor details—if he approves, she can have the story on his desk in two weeks and it will be about 800 words—a word length she knows will be appropriate because she's studied *Baxter Monthly*'s listing in **Writer's Market**. She would not propose a 2,000 word article because they don't publish pieces of that length. And, by the way, Tanya will meet that deadline. Missing a deadline may mean missing your publication opportunity, and it will not impress the editors. Professionals keep their word.

Tanya mentions her publishing credits. *Southern Living* is a well-respected magazine, so that mention would carry some clout. If she had only published in her local paper, Tanya might add, "Tearsheets available upon request," meaning she's willing to send copies of her published work if the editor wants to see them. (A "tearsheet" is literally a page of your published work, as if torn out of a magazine or newspaper.)

When I started writing, query letters contained SASEs (self-addressed, stamped envelopes) for the editor's reply. I usually included an SASP (self-addressed, stamped post-card) upon which I had typed:

_____Yes, please send the article on (whatever I had proposed)

_____ No thanks, not right now.

Why did I send a postcard? It was faster and easier for the editor, plus postcard postage was less expensive for me. Several editors told me they loved the ease and simplicity of my SASP method.

Today, however, I would study the entry in **Writer's Market**. If the magazine requires a query *letter*, I'd enclose a SASP. If they accept emailed queries, I would be sure to include my email beneath my name. It's simple, of course, to click "reply to sender," but the editor may have an intern print all the queries for his perusal, so be sure your email is beneath your name.

Notice what wise Tonya has not done:

- She has not listed every single article she's written or every award she has received.
- She has not suggested that this will be the finest article the editor has ever read.
- She has not offered a type of article the magazine does not publish.
- She has not used profanity; her language is polite and professional.
- She has not implied that her work was dictated by God Himself.
- She has not offered work that is too short or too long for the magazine.
- She has not enclosed or attached the article with the letter. (Some magazines may accept over-the-transom submissions, but those are rare.)

Query letters are not only used for magazine articles, of course. They are also used when you approach an agent and a book publisher. The principles are the same: keep it short, reveal who you are, and briefly describe the project you have in mind.

QUERY LETTER FOR AN AGENT:

Mr. Joe Smith
Literary Agent
Smith and Jones Literary

555 Union Street
Pottersville, NY 12345

Dear Mr. Smith:

I have finished a first draft of a southern novel and am in search of representation. I see from your listing in **Writer's Market** that you represent adult fiction, and I hope you will be willing to look at my proposal.

I am impressed with your client list and would be honored to be among the many fine writers you represent. I have been writing for several years, publishing in magazines and literary collections. I have also written two novellas I would like to eventually publish.

But my heart is wrapped up in *The Offering,* a novel about a Southern woman who discovers that while acting as a surrogate for a childless couple, she inadvertently surrendered her biological child, all that remains of her late husband. The novel will come in at 90,000 words and I can have it completed within six months. I can send an outline and three sample chapters to you within two weeks, should you wish to see my proposal.

Thank you for your time and consideration. I look forward to hearing from you!

Sincerely,
Tanya Wilson
Tanya@gjskbll.com

QUERY LETTER FOR A PUBLISHER

If you wanted to send a proposal to a publisher instead of an agent, the letter would be almost the same. Instead of mentioning the client list (usually available on an agency's website), you could refer to the publisher's catalog, which might also be available on the web.

Be aware, however, that most publishers do not accept proposals unless they come from agents. If you send a proposal to an agent-only publisher, your query letter will probably end up in the trash. This is another situation in which **Writer's Market** will prove invaluable, because the publisher's entry should mention if they accept unagented proposals. If they do, you can send a query letter directly to them.

No matter who you write, make certain every word you write is *the absolute truth*. Don't mention anything you haven't looked up. Write your own letter in your own words. These samples are suggestions, not a form to follow.

If you want to approach a publisher that only accepts queries from agents, what do you do? You get an agent . . . and yes, it can be as difficult to get an agent as it is to get a publisher. But it's possible. For more on that topic, keep reading.

Chapter Four

WRITING FOR PERIODICALS

I'VE ATTENDED AND/OR TAUGHT AT MANY WRITER'S conferences across the country, and I often participate in fifteen minute critique sessions offered to conferees. Yet in all my years of conferring, I have never had anyone ask me for feedback on an article or feature story they were writing —they always want to concentrate on books.

I understand why so many people are eager to publish a book—they might believe that novelists are rich and famous, or that a nonfiction book will establish their credibility in their field.

But writing for magazines also offers valuable rewards. There's money to be made—not a lot, but you could earn more writing ten articles in a week than most novelists would earn during the same week. Writing a feature article can pay between $40-$125 per hour, or between 20 and 30 cents per word.

Writing for magazines also establishes your credibility as a dependable, professional writer. If you have writing clips from ten different magazines, you've worked with at least ten different editors, so you've proven yourself flexible and adaptable. Every magazine has a different audience and a different slant, so you might have written for ten different demographic groups.

Writing for magazines demonstrates that you know how to meet a deadline. Magazines rarely have the luxury of postponing a piece if you can't get the work done, so you've proven your professionalism.

Writing for magazines trains you to think about your reader. Most articles are written to either persuade, challenge, entertain, or call the reader to action. Books should be written with the same purpose, but too many writers write to fulfill their own dreams instead of thinking about the reader's. Books, whether fiction or nonfiction, should be written with the reader in mind. Never forget that.

Small magazines don't pay much, but if you sell an article's *first* serial rights, you can resell that same article to a noncompeting magazine. Or you can tweak the article and sell it to another periodical. When you're pitching a piece, *be sure to mention if the article* has been published elsewhere.

Years ago I interviewed Bill and Gloria Gaither, a husband and wife songwriting duo. They talked about their ministry in music, so I wrote an article about their ministry and sold it to a magazine. During the interview, Gloria mentioned that she had long been fascinated by the potential of the home computer, and she predicted that soon people would be working from home, which could bring about a change in American family life—and this was *before* nearly every home had a computer. I sold an article about Gloria's prediction to yet another periodical.

When you interview someone, record the session as you take notes and let your subject talk freely. You never know what they will reveal, and in the future you may find other ways to use those quotes.

If you live in a college town, as I did, check the college

calendar to see if any celebrities or dignitaries will be visiting the school. If so, get in touch with the guest speaker and see if you can meet with him or her before their speech. Even if you can only get thirty minutes, you can get some strong quotes and you can gather other quotes as you listen to the speech. Whether the guest speaks about education, life's challenges, or the importance of education, you should be able to find a magazine that would be interested in a profile piece.

Do your homework before you show up for the interview. I remember once interviewing Surgeon General Everett Koop. We talked about medicine, then I quietly mentioned that I was sorry he'd recently lost his son in a mountain climbing accident. Those simple and honest words of sympathy meant a lot to him. After his visit, I received a letter from Dr. Koop, thanking me and saying that I was one of the "best-prepared interviewers" he'd ever met.

All because I'd done a little research beforehand . . . and maybe because I treated him like a person, not a mouthpiece.

I have not always prepared properly. Most speakers are happy to be interviewed, but I found out the hard way that you can't take such things for granted. Once a renown prophecy teacher visited my church. Before his arrival, I queried a magazine editor—would she like to see a profile of the man? She said yes.

I knew the teacher would be speaking at the nine and eleven a.m. services, and he would be signing books between services. I thought it'd be simple for him to answer a few of my questions as he signed books.

So there he was, sitting at a little table, signing books, looking a bit bored. I walked over, introduced myself, and said I had a few questions for an article I was writing about him . . .

I don't remember exactly how he replied, but I remember the flash of irritation in his eyes and the words "presumptuous young woman" on his lips. I remember the rush of blood in my ears and the humiliating realization that I had severely over-stepped. I stammered out an apology and backed away.

Presumptuous? He was right.

I slunk into the eleven a.m. service and jotted down a few notes from his sermon. I wrote the article, but it ended up being more about his thoughts on prophecy than on his life.

But it was also good that I learned a lesson. I was completely presumptuous—for the first time, I hadn't prearranged a meeting. I deserved to be utterly and completely embarrassed.

Don't repeat my mistake.

Being a strong interviewer is as simple as being prepared, paying attention, and allowing the conversation to flow freely. Don't be in a hurry to get through your list of questions—sometimes silence gives the subject time to gather his thoughts and say things you might have missed if you'd pressed forward with the next question.

What sort of questions do you ask? You usually approach an interviewee with a request to talk about a certain subject—"I'd like to hear your thoughts on medi-cine," or "I'd like to hear about your days with the circus."

So you will ask questions about the medicine or circus, of course, but don't forget to ask questions that will elicit *stories* from your subject. People love stories.

So ask, "Tell me about a time when you were almost certain you were going to die." Or "Did you fall in love during your circus time? Tell me about it." Or "What was the worst moment of your circus experience, and what situation brought about that moment?"

Don't waste time on esoteric questions like "If you were a tree, what kind of tree would you be?" Instead ask questions that will elicit memories, opinions, and practical speculation: "If you had not joined the circus, how would you be different today?"

Remember to actively listen to your subject, take notes, and monitor your recorder. More than once I had my recorder fail, and frantically had to fill in the gaps of my notes so I'd have enough useable material for the article. What can go wrong usually *does* go wrong . . .

FROM NOTES TO FINISHED ARTICLE

When it comes to writing up the interview, most writers simply type out the subject's answers, and introduce the quotes with brief transition lines, like this:

> When asked about how his life would be different if he'd never joined the circus, John says, "I wouldn't have visited as many different places, that's for sure."

That sort of simple writing works, but it's nothing special and there's no guarantee it will be accepted by an editor. But you can easily make your work rise above the slush pile. I learned how after reading an article on physical action in *Writer's Digest* magazine. So in my next article, I interspersed **physical action** amid the quotes.

About a week after I handed in that profile piece, the editor called me. "What did you *do?*" she asked. "The article is *so* much better than your usual interviews."

I laughed and told her about how I'd interviewed then-Secretary of Education William Bennett. In my research,

I'd discovered that he had recently become a father. I had to share my interview time with a lady from the local TV station, so we both sat and listened to him talk about education, etc., etc. The photographer with us had snapped a few shots, but it was a fairly unremarkable interview.

Because time was running out, I jumped in. "I know you have a young son," I said. "Tell me what it's like to be a new father."

Bennett sprang to life. His eyes sparkled as he leaned forward in his chair. As a small smile curved his mouth, he talked about his little boy. The photographer jumped up and started shooting again because we were seeing a different side of William Bennett.

I wrote up the profile with the same sort of description I used in the above paragraph, surrounding his quotes with descriptions of his body language. It's a fiction technique, but it helps nonfiction come to life. The reader can *see* the interviewee.

So evoke more of your readers' senses when they read your piece. Let them see the subject, let them hear the snap of his chewing gum (if appropriate), and feel the warmth of his smile. Make your subject come to life with a sprinkling of physical description.

If you did a telephone interview, however, you'll be limited to describing the subject's voice, noting pauses and hesitations, and describing laughter and tone. Trickier, but still possible.

Some interviews are done on paper—writers submit a list of questions and the subject (or an assistant) emails them to the writer. If at all possible, avoid this method because it doesn't allow you to observe your subject. Suggest that the interview occur over the phone or, better yet, over Zoom. You and your subject will be better served if you can observe the person you're interviewing.

Magazines buy many different types of articles, so if you find the thought of doing an interview intimidating, you could write humor, a nostalgia piece, a how-to, a personal experience piece—the list is endless. Consult **Writer's Market**, determine what sort of articles your favorite magazines purchase, and learn how to write that kind of article. How? Google: "how to write (fill in the blank) article."

Every sort of writing has its own blueprint, so do the research and get started on the writing. Using **Writer's Market,** jot down several magazines that purchase the sort of article you have written. Send a query letter to the first magazine and get busy writing. If that first magazine passes, try another. And another.

I created a "submission sheet" for my articles. I put the name of the article on top, then kept a numbered list of the magazines I sent it to. When my SASP came back, I made a note of the response: if it sold, I noted which rights were purchased (first, second, or reprint), and I'd get busy writing. If the editor passed, I sent the query out again, pitching the idea to a different magazine.

I usually had at least two dozen articles under consideration at all times—which probably explains why saving money on postage was important to me.

As I sent out those queries, editors began to recognize my name. I became a known entity, not a stranger. And you know what? In time, I stopped pitching article ideas because editors were contacting me with assignments. The editor or the editorial board had come up with an idea and they needed someone dependable and competent to write it.

That, dear reader, could be you.

Chapter Five

GETTING AN AGENT

How do you find and engage an agent? I have a good news/bad news answer.

The bad news is that it can be as difficult to get a good agent as it is to get a publisher.

The good news is that once you have an agent, the doors that were closed to unagented writers will open to you.

That's not the only good news. Agents do so much to help a writer. They can read your manuscripts and offer editorial advice (as a rule, however, they do not edit your manuscript). Agents negotiate on your behalf, allowing you to stay out of the fray. Agents care about your long-term career, not just the next book. By investing in your success, they are investing in their own. Agents know more about the market and *other writer's deals* than you do. They are not going to tell you what their other clients are earning—that would be a breach of trust—but they know what a fair offer looks like.

Agents know about subsidiary rights, foreign markets, and fine print. Agents aren't afraid to walk away from a lousy deal, because sometimes you should and new writers are reluctant to do it. Agents know about auctions and advertising and other agents.

How does the agent-author relationship work? Once you sign a contract with an agent, you agree to let him or her represent you in all your book deals until the agency agreement is terminated. And even if that agreement is terminated, that agent will continue to represent all the books he or she negotiated until the book contract ends— i.e., when the book goes out of print and rights revert to the author.

If you sign a contract with Joe Smith to represent you and he sells your book *My Favorite Dog* to a publisher called Bad to the Bone Books, Joe will earn 15 percent of every payout you receive until *My Favorite Dog* is out of print, even if you terminate your agreement with Joe next year. That's only fair: he did the work to represent you and negotiate that deal, so he deserves to be paid for his work on that deal for as long as the deal exists. When that book contract ends, however, so does Joe's share of the earnings.

Consider the contract for *My Favorite Dog*—the contract Joe negotiated. The contract says you will receive a $10,000 advance in royalties. That means Bad to the Bone Books will either send Joe a check for $10,000 and he will send you $8500 after he's taken out his 15 percent, or the publisher will send Joe a check for $1500 and you a check for $8500. The latter method is more common these days, and it's far better for the author. Most publishers wait thirty days after the contract is finalized before sending the check, so why should you wait even longer for Joe to send your portion? Most publishers are happy to send separate checks: one to the agent; one to the author.

When *My Favorite Dog* goes out of print, if you receive a letter from the publisher saying that rights have reverted to you, you are free to either sell the book again (a long shot, even with an agent's help) or self-publish it. Some agents are happy to help their authors with self-publishing for a fee or commission; other writers prefer to do the work themselves. Self-publishing *is* work: someone must format the manuscript, design a cover and interior pages, acquire the ISBN, and place the manuscript with a printer, so it's not a simple task.

I sold several books without an agent and quickly realized that I needed someone to help me keep track of royalty statements and when I should expect royalty payments. I also needed general career advice. I hired a two-man agency and they did a great job for me. A few years down the road, however, one of the agents decided to take another job. The remaining agent kept representing the works they had sold for me, but advised me to find another agent for new work.

So I went to the biggest agency in New York—William Morris. I found a wonderful young woman there to act as my agent, and we had a warm relationship. But being a small fish in a huge pond has its drawbacks. Whenever I received a new contract, it had to go through the legal department at William Morris, and that seemed to take forever. My editors were ready to move forward, I was ready to move, but I always seemed to be waiting on the legal department . . .

Regretfully, I terminated that agent's contract and went with a smaller Christian agency, since most of my books were for the Christian market. They helped me get writing work I wouldn't have been offered if I'd stayed with William Morris, but who knows the opposite isn't true as well? Life is a series of considered choices. At every decision point, you say "yes" to some opportunities and "no" to others.

A few years later, an upheaval at that agency caused me to search for another agent, so this time I made an Excel chart and listed several characteristics that were important to me. These are the criteria I remember:

- returns my phone calls
- seems enthusiastic about my work
- represents the general and the Christian market
- has other long-term clients (so he or she is not likely to quit next week)
- charges the standard fee (currently 15 percent)
- does not charge a reading fee (*no* reputable agent will charge to read your manuscript)
- friendly; we can get along
- handles and sells foreign rights
- can handle film rights
- is a member of the Association of American Literary Agents (members of that group adhere to a set code of ethics: https://aalitagents.org/canon-of-ethics/)

I called several agents, scored them in each area, and added up the scores. This method may sound a little crazy, but it worked for me, even though it was a close call. I've been with my current agent for more years than I can count.

The author-agent relationship is somewhat like a marriage—there's an emotional investment from both partners, and breaking up is not easy, especially if the decision isn't mutual. A strong agent-author relationship should be based on respect, honesty, and friendship.

While your agent is a friend, he or she shouldn't be your *best* friend. Keep the relationship professional, and do not demand so much of your agent's time that she has no time for other clients or a personal life.

When you are first looking for an agent, you may feel as though the agent is evaluating *you*—and you'd be right. If agents had an Excel chart like mine, it might have criteria like these:

- Is the client going to phone me every single day?
- Does the client write well?
- Does the client understand how the publishing business works?
- Is this client going to demand too much of my time?
- Is this client emotionally needy?
- Does this client expect me to make her rich?
- Is this client going to undercut my efforts by becoming *too* involved?
- Does this client write in only one genre?
- Does this client demonstrate flexibility?
- Can this client ride out the ups and downs of the writing life?
- Is this client interested in a long term career?

Respect the agents you interview and the one who will represent you. They are working for your benefit as well as theirs.

When you first hear that an agent wants to represent you, you may feel that you've just won the lottery. But always remember that your agent works *for you*. If your agent isn't returning your calls, forwarding your payments, or giving you timely feedback about manuscript submissions, it might be time to look for a new agent.

Agents make money when they sell manuscripts, so they are highly motivated to make submissions and negotiate deals. But to do that, they need well-written, polished novels and nonfiction books. They need timely topics and emotionally moving stories. They need writers who are serious about doing the work. They don't want to waste their time with something that won't sell.

Some agents specialize; that's why you should search *Writer's Market* for a list of agents and what they represent. Most handle general market fiction and nonfiction; others will handle children's books, gift books, and other specialty products. Most Hollywood agents handle screenplays. You can also start on the home page of the Association of American Literary Agents (https://aalitagents.org) and search for an agent based upon what you write.

A movie producer once put an option on my novel *The Note*. My agent at the time went over the option and film contract and saw no red flags.

For five years the producer tried to raise the money to turn *The Note* into a theatrical release, but finally ended up selling his option to a company who produced it as a Hallmark movie. That movie was so popular that the company made two sequels . . . and though they used my characters, I didn't receive a penny for the sequels. But they did pay me to write a novella based on the second movie's screenplay. That work did help me pay a few bills, but the resulting book was nothing like my other novels, and readers have noticed.

A few years ago I had another novel optioned for film, and my current agent recommended that I hire a Hollywood agent (she supplied a name) to go over the contract. "She's more familiar with the terms," my agent explained. And she was. In the new contract, I noticed that the payment for sequels was spelled out.

You can't expect your agent to be an expert about *every* area, so if you find yourself dealing with Hollywood or some other speciality market, don't be shy about hiring an expert to review your contract agreement. Just make sure your agent knows what you're doing.

There are certain protocols you should be aware of when dealing with an agent. First, agents are not supposed to woo other agents' clients. If you are represented and *another* agent tries to persuade you to leave your current agency—well, that's not acceptable behavior.

An agent is supposed to maintain confidentiality. If you confide in your agent about a matter, you should be able to trust that your secret won't be spread throughout the industry.

Likewise, you should never go behind your agent's back. When an agent represents you, the contract will likely say that he or she will represent every written work you sell until the agreement is terminated. Technically, that means *anything* you sell—books, magazine articles, children's books, etc. But if your agent doesn't want to keep track of magazine articles or children's books, just run that by him or her before you start negotiating with a publisher for a picture book.

You are the boss in the agent/writer relationship, but the agent is the expert, so listen carefully to his or her advice. Because your agent has a deep knowledge of the industry, you will be free to write the best books you can write.

If and when you feel that the arrangement isn't working, be up front and honest. Have a conversation, terminate the contract if necessary, and remember that the agent will remain the agent of record on any contracts he or she negotiated.

The book industry is always changing, and agents are changing, too. As I mentioned, many agencies now play a role in helping their authors self-publish out of print titles.

Many actively sell foreign, audio, and film rights. Many specialize, so if you write outside their chosen area, you're free to sell those works yourself—but you should let your agent know what you're doing.

So when you are searching for an agent, do your research, conduct some interviews, and ask appropriate questions. You want to establish a solid working relationship that will last for years and be mutually beneficial.

Because breaking up is hard to do.

Chapter Six

HOW BOOK PUBLISHING WORKS

Selling to magazines and other periodicals is fairly straightforward—you query the editor, send in the manuscript if requested, and wait to hear if the company will be purchasing all rights, first serial rights, second rights, or reprint rights. In time, often on publication, you receive a check and a copy of your published article.

Book publishing, on the other hand, is more time intensive. Many companies will not take unagented proposals, so you have to get an agent, who will guide you in the creation of a stellar proposal. If this is your first book, you may have to write the entire book in order to get a contract—and that's okay, because once you've proven that you can finish a manuscript, you probably won't have to do it again. Your future contracts will be awarded on the basis of a proposal and sample chapters, because you've already proven that you can finish a book (you'd be surprised at how many writers can't).

THE CONTRACT

Let's say you have sent in a manuscript and your agent calls with happy news. They are sending deal points for a contract, and your agent will negotiate the points such as:

*due date for completed manuscript
*royalty rate
*the option clause, if any
*the rights reversion clause, if any
*due dates for any other books included in the contract
*subsidiary rights

Let's look at these individually.

The manuscript you hand in will not be the final version of your book. Even if you hand in a complete manuscript, it won't be "delivered and accepted" until the acquiring editor says it is. Your manuscript will go through a substantive edit, so you will be revising it. Some revisions are light; others are intensive. But your editor will give you reasoned suggestions to help your manuscript be the best it can possibly be. She will also give you a due date. Publishing operates on a strict schedule, and if you miss your deadline, you could throw off the entire chain of events, delaying the publication of your book for months.

The following has been greatly simplified, but contains the information an author needs to know:

After the manuscript leaves the **editorial department,** it goes to the **art department** for design, the cover, the formatting, and other artistic aspects. Simultaneously, the book is being evaluated by the **marketing** department, who will plan a marketing campaign and decide the best way to advertise your book. Years ago, marketing was all about print ads. Today the emphasis is on social media.

The **sales team** will also learn about your book, and the **catalog creators** will prepare an ad for your book. You may be asked to supply copy and a brief bio for inclusion on this page.

Every publisher is different, but most generally take a year to produce a book. When I hand in a manuscript, I do not expect to hold the finished book until several months have passed.

Back to the contract:

The royalty rate: these can vary, so I'm not even going to attempt to guess at what your royalty rate might be. Some publishers offer a royalty off the retail price, others figure royalty off the net price (the price the publisher gets from the bookstore, which is usually *at least* 40 percent less than retail). Bookstores often buy at discounts of 50-55 percent off retail, especially if the book is expected to be a best seller. No wonder writers are most concerned about the amount of the advance—the royalty is unpredictable.

The option clause: If there is an option clause, it will usually say something like "Publisher reserves the right to exercise a purchase option on the author's next book . . ."

This clause, as stated, is heavily slanted in favor of the publisher. Suppose the book they buy is a romance, but your next book is going to be a memoir about life with your dog. You have a strong hunch they are not the ideal publisher for a dog memoir. The solution is simple: have your agent amend that clause so it reads: "Publisher reserves the right to exercise a purchase option on the author's next romance."

It's fair to give them a first look at your next romance,

since that's what they're buying at the moment. Limiting the option to romances, however, leaves you free to write something else, should you choose to do so.

The rights reversion clause: these used to be standard, but many publishers are now leaving them out, figuring that ebooks never go out of print. But this is not really fair to authors. You can write a book and the publisher can stop selling it in paper, stop advertising it, and even stop listing it in their catalog. How can it sell if no one knows about it? If you could get the rights back, you could self-publish it, give it a new cover, and republish it yourself . . . but you can't do that unless the rights have reverted from the former publisher.

The fairest rights reversion clauses are based on sales numbers. The language could read like this: "If sales of (insert title here) slow to less than $200 per year, author has the right to ask for a rights reversion, which will be granted."

That is fair and logical, but not all publishers are willing to agree. Have you agent do his or her best to get a fair rights reversion clause inserted into your contract.

Due dates for other books: wait, more than one book? Yes. Even though you proposed only one book, many publishers will look at you as an investment. If you are a new author, they will be investing in you and establishing your name, so they *may* want you to commit to two or three books. It's a reasonable request, and one that may benefit you as well. The advance will now cover all the books on the contract, and each book will be assigned its own deadline. Make sure the deadlines give you plenty of time to honor your commitment.

Subsidiary rights: Each publisher's standard contract is different, but among other details you may find clauses for book club deals (the organizations that buy a title and send it to all their subscribers), subsidiary rights (in case someone wants to do a book of paper dolls based on your characters, for instance), other media rights, foreign rights, audio rights, film rights, serial rights, and moral turpitude clauses.

Your agent may want to keep the foreign and/or audio rights, if he or she regularly sells to those outlets, but the publisher will want to keep as many rights as possible. But experience has taught me that most publishers excel at selling books . . . and many agents do better with the other rights.

Your agent should discuss each area of the contract with you and help you understand any areas that need to be reconsidered or negotiated.

Just remember this: the publisher wants most of the clauses to favor *them*. The author wants the deal points to favor *him*. But publishing is a shared risk, and the publisher is the entity with the most at risk.

So do your best to be reasonable and agreeable.

THE EDITING

Once your editor has had a chance to read your manuscript, you will receive a letter describing ways the manuscript can be improved—this process is the *substantive edit*. He or she will not usually correct misspellings or grammar because this is a "big picture" edit, not a copy or line edit. Instead, the fiction editor may make suggestions about character, genre, plausibility, and/or plot development. The nonfiction editor will make suggestions about the material's organization, readability, and depth of coverage. The editor will not mark up a manuscript line by line but may make comments in a letter and/or in the digital copy of the manuscript. This is likely to be the most important edit of your book.

A word here about working with your editor—when you first read the notes that arrive after your substantive edit, the human reaction is to be defensive. You've done your best, you've worked hard, so how could the manuscript *possibly* need more work?

If necessary, set aside those editorial notes and take a day or two for your emotions to settle. Then read those notes again, reminding yourself that you and the editor are a team. Your common goal is to make this book the best it can be. The editor is thinking like a reader, and you are so close to the work you can't be objective.

So take a deep breath and go through the editor's suggestions, making changes as needed to improve the book. You'll be glad you did.

Most of the time, I agree with my editor's changes. Every manuscript can benefit from another pair of eyes and a fresh perspective.

But what if the editor is absolutely wrong about something? It may be that your editor has missed your point, and if that's so, perhaps you didn't make your point effectively. But here's the bottom line: *choose your battles carefully*. The expert editor is not going to be wrong about everything. He or she is most likely right to make those suggestions, and you will benefit if you make the suggested changes.

Whenever an editor questions me, I make an attempt to make my case. If my case is persuasive—if I have a strong reason for doing whatever the editor questioned—I'm usually allowed to let my choice remain.

For instance—in *The Note,* one of my novels, the newspaper reporter protagonist's point of view is written in third person: "She went into the room and picked up her purse," etc.

But in four or five scenes, I had minor characters

address the reader like this: "Peyton? I think she's an odd duck. I mean, she's nice enough, but there seems to be something beneath the surface, you know?"

My editor questioned those scenes. Why did I have those characters "break the fourth wall?"

I told her that I envisioned the story as a documentary of sorts, and those were occasions when the people around Peyton spoke directly to the reader. Since Peyton was a closed-off sort of person, those characters gave the reader important insights.

My editor let me keep that approach, and never has a single reader mentioned that it was unusual.

So listen to your editor. By the way *stet* is Latin for "let it stand." If you are going through edits on paper, use stet to tell the editor to leave your phrase as it was. But use stet rarely, not on every change.

Throughout the editing process, be kind, not disgruntled. Aim to be the kind of writer editors will enjoy working with. It's a collaboration, after all.

After you have revised your manuscript again, the editor will review your changes and begin the copy or line edit. (A different editor may do this work.) The copy editor will work through your manuscript, checking line by line, marking obvious mistakes (misspellings, bad grammar, contradictions, implausibilities) and rephrasing where necessary for clarity. When self-publishing writers hire editors, they usually get a copy edit (when perhaps they needed a substantive edit).

After the copy edit, the manuscript may be sent back to you. I usually receive my copyedited manuscripts as Word documents, with track changes on so the changes have been highlighted. I read through the manuscript quickly, and only hesitate when a change either makes no sense, is wrong, or changes my original meaning. My current copy editor knows me, so I rarely stet anything he has changed.

After I send back the manuscript yet again, the document goes to the proofreader, and after that it is printed on first pages, or galleys. Galleys used to be long sheets of paper but now they are usually printed on regular 8.5 x 11 sheets or may even be digital. Writers are usually sent the galleys for "one last look" before the book goes to the printer. As the writer reads over the copy, the publisher's proofreaders will also be checking it. Writers are urged to avoid making any major changes at this point, but to highlight any typos, bad breaks in a hyphenated word, inconsistent formatting, etc.

(If you are self-publishing, the manuscript you upload should have already been through this process—you should have had your manuscript edited and proofed, because you are technically uploading the galley. Ingram Spark will send you a digital proof with the cover for you to check, and Amazon KDP lets you preview the document online. Don't ignore this step—for some reason, errors tend to be more obvious when we're looking at them on a formatted page. If you find a mistake, fix it in the original file, upload it again, and repeat the process. You can fix mistakes later, but it's much easier to repair them at the proof stage.)

Once the pages have been approved by everyone, the book goes to the printer. Meanwhile, you should get busy writing your next book while the marketing department is lining up blog tours, sending review copies out to reviewers, and preparing catalog copy for the company catalog.

Finally, months after you sent the book in, you receive a copy or two for yourself. The release date may still be a month away, but you are finally able to hold your new baby. I've published loads of books, but this moment is still priceless.

Then the book comes out, and you see that it is available on Amazon, Barnes & Noble, and other online retailers. You send out an email telling friends and family about your new release, then you go back to your room and keep typing.

Because you have another book to finish, and it won't write itself.

Chapter Seven

HOW DO WRITERS GET PAID?

FREELANCE WRITERS ARE COMPLETELY IN CHARGE OF their own careers. You choose who you want to work for, when you want to work, and what you'll wear when you're working. You usually have a home office, though you can work pretty much anywhere.

With all that freedom comes responsibility. You collect a check after you've finished a job, you deposit it in your company's bank account, and you are responsible for paying your own business bills, buying your own supplies, and paying your own taxes—including the employer's half of self-employment taxes. You are the employer now, so get used to the idea of wearing two hats—the employee's and the employer's. Unless you have a spouse with a family health insurance plan, you'll have to cover medical expenses, too.

To operate as a business, set up a separate bank account in your business name. Get an EIN (employer identification number)[1] from the IRS. Pay all business expenses from your company account and put all income into that account. All checks should be endorsed with a company stamp that says, "For Deposit Only." The money you pay yourself as salary will come out of your business account.

Getting paid as a writer requires patience. Most companies pay on time, but if a contract says you'll be paid thirty days after signing, you probably won't see a check until that thirty days has passed.

Occasionally you will have a client who cannot or will not pay. It's easier to forgive a small debt than a large one, but sometimes the hassle and expense of hiring a lawyer is more trouble than it's worth. The legal department of the Author's Guild may be able to assist you with contract reviews, copyright issues, and business disputes, but you must join the AG in order to request help from their lawyers.

When you write for a client like an advertising agency, most of the time you submit an invoice for the time worked (set an hourly rate) and get paid immediately. When you write for a magazine, you will often be paid on publication, which means you may wait months for a check. It's easy to forget about those checks, so make a note on your calendar so you can follow up if payment doesn't arrive when it should. A friendly email to follow up on a missing check is not out of line.

Some magazines pay by the word, some by the job. **Writer's Market** usually specifies which.

When you write for a book publisher, you receive the advance after signing the contract—usually one-third 30 days after signing, another third upon acceptance of the

---

1. https://www.irs.gov/businesses/small-businesses-self-employed/apply-for-an-employer-identification-number-ein-online

manuscript (after you've done the requested revisions), and another third thirty days after publication. If your check doesn't arrive when it's supposed to, have your agent send an email to follow up.

After your book is published, you should receive royalty statements on a regular schedule. Some companies pay royalties every quarter, some every six months, some once a year. Each time you should receive a statement showing how many of your books were sold and in which formats (ebook, paperback, hardcover, and any subsidiary editions such as large print or book club editions). Remember, you will not receive any additional payments until the advance has "earned out"—until your royalties surpass the amount of your advance (including the amount you paid your agent). Your royalty statement will show how much your book earned and how much of the advance remains unearned. When your royalties surpass the amount of your advance, you will find a check included with your royalty statement.

Work-for-hire projects: Suppose you collaborate with a celebrity and write his book. You will most likely not receive royalties, but a flat fee: half upon signing the work for hire contract, and half upon delivery and acceptance of the completed manuscript. I have done several work for hire collaborations and I've enjoyed all of them. Not everyone is a writer, so these are a way to use your skills and help someone else tell their story.

Ghostwriting is usually work for hire. I used to ghost-write, but after reading an essay by Randy Alcorn[2] about the deception inherent in such ventures, I no longer do— and I'm not the only writer who finds the deception

---

2. To read Randy's essay: https://www.epm.org/resources/2020/Feb/3/ethics-ghostwriting/

disturbing. What does it cost someone to admit they had help with their book? Nothing but a little pride. I'm happy to write someone else's story (with their cooperation, of course), but my name has to be on the project somewhere. Even on the title page in teeny tiny letters. I'm not fussy, but I do try to be honest.

Three times I've been asked to take a screenplay and turn it into a novel—which[3] is not as easy as it sounds. A screenplay turned into prose is only about 25,000 words, and the average novel should be at least 70,000. So a novelist must not only be true to the story but must "fill in the canvas" with sights, sounds, textures, and backstory that did not make it into the script. Since the work is based on someone else's plot and characters, such novelizations are usually work-for-hire. The writer is paid for doing the work, but royalties are not usually part of the deal.

Writers are asked to write all kinds of things—plays, school programs, church musicals, and neighborhood newsletters. Share your talent with your favorite causes and don't worry about payment for those jobs—some things we do for the love of it. You may also write some projects "on spec" (speculation) because you're hoping to sell the work in the future. I recently wrote a Passover Play with a musician friend and as of this writing we haven't found a publisher for our musical drama. But we're still hoping.

You will write some things for love and some for work. But if you want to make a career out of writing, you'll need to find the right balance and be smart about the financial aspects of writing.

Time to get down to the nitty gritty.

---

3. My projects were *Risen, The Nativity Story,* and *Paul, Apostle of Christ.*

Chapter Eight

HOW MUCH DO WRITERS EARN?

I WAS ONCE SPEAKING TO SOME ELEMENTARY SCHOOL KIDS who were excited about meeting "a famous author." I let them ask questions, and will never forget when a handsome young man raised his hand and asked, "So—are you just *swimming* in money?"

Rather that quote the figures I'll get to in a minute, I held up one of my picture books. "This book sells for about $15 in the store," I said. "How much of that do you think I get?"

The numbers started flying: "Seven dollars! Five dollars! Ten dollars!" Finally I quieted them and told them the truth: "I get about twenty-five cents."

Their faces fell. I explained that the bookstore had to pay its bills and employees, the publisher had to pay the editors, designers, marketers, warehouse people, salesmen, and administrators. Also, because it was a picture book, the author's share was cut in half so the artist could be paid, too.

However, writers who publish independently earn much more per book because they don't have to pay the warehouse people, salesmen, and administrators. Those who self-publish should pay editors and designers and marketers (if they want to produce and actually sell a quality book), but the royalty rate is higher. For instance, Amazon's KDP program offers a 70 percent royalty option for ebooks, and you, the author, are able to choose the royalty rate and purchase price. Therefore you actually set the amount of royalty you will receive per book. With independent publishing you'll earn more per sale, but you are likely to sell fewer books. We'll talk more about this later.

Here's the hard truth: to make loads of money in writing, you have to sell loads of books. Paint that on a poster and hang it on your wall, especially if you tend to dream of mansions in Beverly Hills.

Yep, some folks get rich, but most don't. Here are the most current statistics I've read, from an Authors' Guild survey:

"The median author income for **full-time authors** from their books was $10,000 in 2022, and their total median earnings from their book and other author-related income combined was $20,000. Book income includes advances, royalties, and fees from licensing and subsidiary rights. Other author-related income includes work such as editing, blogging, teaching, speaking, book coaching, copy writing and journalism.

"When looking at **full-time authors** whose books are in **commercial** markets (i.e, excluding academic, scholarly, and educational books), the median book income was $15,000 and median author-related income was $25,000.

"This means half of all full-time authors continue to earn below minimum wage in many states from *all* their writing related work, and well below the federal minimum wage of just $7.25/hour from their books. It also tells us that most authors are earning half of their writing-related income from sources other than their books.

"The median book income for **all** authors (including those who write part-time) who completed the survey (80 percent of whom consider themselves professional authors, but only 35 percent of whom considered themselves full time), was just \$2,000 for 2022, and the median total writing-related income was \$5,000."

You can read the full report here: https://authorsguild.org/news/key-takeaways-from-2023-author-income-survey/

Do those figures surprise you? Now—repeat what I told you to hang on the wall: *to make loads of money in writing, you have to sell loads of books.* How do you sell loads of books? By writing irresistible stories. By learning the craft. By winning readers one at a time. By working *hard.*

And don't forget—being a writer is like being a builder. If you learn how to use the tools, you can write anything as long as you follow the appropriate blueprint. So if you want a writing career, branch out! Work on your book, write some articles, do some interviews. Write this and that and stretch yourself. You'll grow in knowledge and experience, plus you'll gain credibility and lots of published clips! It's the way to earn while you learn. I got started this way, and you can, too.

Here's the hard truth: not every writer is destined to be as rich as Stephen King. A lot of writers are working hard to earn a living and must find other ways to supplement their income. Many rely on the income of a spouse, especially in the "getting started" years. Many have nine-to-five jobs and write early in the morning or late at night.

Some glamorous writer's life, right? Actually . . . it can be. Because when you sit down at the computer, you forget about everything but the writing, and off you go to ancient

Rome or the rain forest or medieval Ireland, where the adventure of a lifetime is waiting.

Chapter Nine

HOW MUCH SHOULD YOU CHARGE?

FREELANCE WRITERS OFTEN ASK HOW MUCH THEY SHOULD charge for various projects. I can't quote a number because there are too many variables. Writers who are multi-published and more experienced can charge more, and writers who are just beginning might want to donate their efforts to gain some publishing credits. Add inflation to those uncertainties, and anyone would find it difficult to set a specific price for certain jobs.

Writer's Market, however, does list suggested prices in its annual volume, so I suggest you buy a copy and keep it handy. Those suggested prices (which are usually a range) will help you establish a starting point when you're asked to write a piece or edit someone's work.

For instance, if someone hires you to write a feature article for a magazine:

If you charge by the hour, the scale ranges from $15 to $194.

If you charge by the project, the scale ranges from $25 to $8,000.

If you charge by the word, the scale ranges from 10 cents a word to $3.00 a word.

(For most magazines, the compensation is predetermined and quoted in their **Writer's Market** listing. But if you are given an assignment, the price could be negotiable.).

What about collaboration? Often two people want to write a book together, or one person wants to contribute the idea while the other person does the writing. Or perhaps one person will supply the expertise or the marketing or the famous name while the other person writes.

I don't mean to demean the expertise or marketing prowess of the non-writing partner, but if the writing fails, the book will fail. Any partnership of a writer and non-writer should be at least a 50-50 split, and perhaps slanted more toward the writer—60/40 sounds better.

Note: I am being completely idealistic here. But if I am completely *realistic*, if my agent said that John Grisham wanted to write a book with me as a Grisham /Hunt 70/30 percent split, I'd accept the deal. Why? Because 30 percent of a Grisham book would be enough to keep me happy.

But let's get back to regular people:

If two people are *both* planning to write, a 50-50 split is fair unless one of the partners will also act as editor, which requires additional work.

Perhaps your collaborative venture is a labor of love and the split doesn't matter. In that case, divide the expenses and profits evenly and carry on.

But whatever you do, settle these details and the deadline before you begin to write. Participants should be equally committed so the book gets done. When the work is finished, together you can decide whether you want to submit it to traditional publishers or self-publish.

A note about children's books—many times someone will write a children's story, then ask a friend or relative to do the illustrations before submitting the package to a children's publisher. That's a mistake. Picture book manuscripts should be submitted *alone* because publishers want to find the best artist for the story, and they are likely to have wider contacts (and budgets) than you do. The exception to this rule is an author who is also an accomplished artist.

So . . . how much should you charge? Most of the time, the writer's compensation is predetermined. You accept it, reject it, or try to negotiate a better price.

If the compensation has not been predetermined, consult **Writer's Market** and choose a point on the scale that reflects your ability and experience.

Chapter Ten

ESTABLISHING YOUR BUSINESS

LEAVING THE TOPIC OF MONEY, LET'S TALK ABOUT structure. You have many options about how to organize your business, and the choice depends on what is best for you and your family.

Let me say up front that I'm not a CPA, a tax expert, or a lawyer. But I can give you the following guidelines and urge you to confirm your choices with your accountant or financial advisor.

I've already mentioned that you should open a separate checking account in the name of your company. Your publisher should write checks to your business name, not your personal name.

Expenses are paid from the company account and income goes into that account. Since writers are paid at irregular intervals, you might want to discipline yourself to take only a small amount of income as your salary. A writer's income is often a "feast or famine" situation, so try to avoid splurging during the feast and set some money aside for the famine.

SOLE PROPRIETOR

Your first option: run your business as a self-employed sole proprietor and file a schedule C at tax time. The easiest option is to record your writing income and deductions on your schedule C.

Dedicate one room in your home for use as your office (it has to be your *full-time office* not used for any other purpose), and figure the square feet. Subtract the area of that room from your home's total square footage and come up with the percentage.

If your office space is 10 percent of your home's square footage, you can deduct ten percent of your utility bills, homeowner's insurance, exterminator, and real estate taxes as business expenses. You can also deduct any books you buy for research, movies you rent for research or inspiration, mileage for trips to the library, to research an old building, or to visit your accountant. You can deduct all expenses for office supplies like paper, ink, and notebooks. Your computer, printer, even a camera can all be legitimate business expenses.

Subtract your deductions from your income, and the result is your net self-employed income. You'll have to pay the employer's half of social security taxes on that amount.

INCORPORATION

If you want to, you can incorporate your business as an LLC, an S corporation, or a C corporation.

People often choose to incorporate in order to shield themselves from the liability of being sued because of something they wrote. For instance, if someone named Joe Smith claims you've slandered him by creating a murderer in your mystery *Joe Smith Returns*, Joe could sue the corporation (provided the corporation holds the copyright), but he couldn't sue you.

In all my years, I have never heard of any writer being sued because of a character's name. Doesn't mean it has never happened, though, because anyone can sue anyone for virtually anything.

But the reason incorporation is valued is because LLCs, S corps, and C corporations offer *limited liability protection*— you are not personally liable for the business's debts or obligations.

An LLC is simple and similar to an S corp because income is reported on the owner's tax return. You won't have to maintain records of corporate meetings, but you will have to pay a state fee each year—check with your state to determine the requirements for a single member LLC.

If you file as an S corporation, your business profits will be run through your personal taxes, saving you from double taxation. You will file an annual 1120 S, quarterly form 941 to transmit withheld income and social security taxes, and an annual 940, to pay unemployment taxes.

If you file as a C corp, you will file and pay your personal taxes and your corporation will file its own taxes. Like the S corp, a C corp will file an annual form 1120, quarterly forms 941 to transmit income and other employment taxes, and an annual form 940. C corps are also required to have annual shareholders meetings—if you're the only shareholder, you can take yourself out to dinner and have your meeting at a wonderful restaurant.

If you incorporate as a schedule C, profits from the corporation will be taxed at the federal corporate tax rate, which can be higher than a personal tax rate. But notice the word *profit*. If your corporation spends all its income by paying expenses, salary, and employee benefits, there should be no profit, so you would owe no corporate taxes.

People often point out, correctly, that C corps are subject to double taxation—you, as owner, would be taxed on the corporation's profits and then again for your personal taxes because you took a salary. But since the corporation is taxed only on profits, my goal has always been to empty the coffers. I'm usually successful.

Establishing a corporation requires filing paperwork with the federal and state governments. You can do this yourself or hire a lawyer to walk you through the process, but it's a simple matter.

I used the excellent book *Inc. Yourself* by Judith McQuown to educate myself about corporations.[1] Make sure to purchase the latest edition because tax laws are always changing.

I chose a C corp, and I'll tell you why. First, since my goal has always been not to make a profit, I don't worry about double taxation.

Second, when I incorporated many years ago, my kids were young. Under a C corp, I was able to establish a medical reimbursement plan *for all my employees and their family members* (I had one employee: me) that covered all our health expenses and dental expenses, including orthodontia. My husband had health insurance through his employer, but my company paid all the deductibles and medical expenses his plan didn't cover, including braces for both kids.

My corporation bought my car and paid for my auto insurance. My corporation paid rent to my family for the home office that occupied 25 percent of my house (including the garage space that housed the company car). I

---

1. Buy Inc. Yourself

had to report that income on our personal taxes, of course, but it was offset by deductions for repairs, maintenance, the exterminator—any house expense my company *wasn't* paying. You can't deduct the same expense from personal income *and* company income.

Why are those things a big deal? I would still have to pay those bills if I used my own money, right?

Not quite. I paid for the car and the braces and medical bills with **corporate** dollars, which were not taxed. Pre-tax dollars are worth more than taxed dollars. If I had paid for them from my personal account, I would have had to pay with money I'd earned as my salary, which would have been taxed. So the amount of personal money I had to spend would have been x percentage (insert tax rate here) less.

If financial talk confuses you (sometimes it makes me crazy!), let's boil it down to basics. If my corporation pays my $200 medical bill, I personally will pay nothing. And that bill will be another deduction that keeps my corporation from making a profit.

But if my tax rate is 20 percent and I paid the $200 medical bill from *personal* (taxed) money, I would have to earn $240 to pay that bill.

When you add all the savings from years of paying employment benefits with corporate dollars, you can see that being a C corp made a big difference to my growing family—and it might for yours, too.

How do you decide if you earn enough to bother with incorporation? Talk to your accountant or financial advisor. If your earnings and deductions are small in the early years, you will probably want to remain a sole proprietor, but once you begin to earn more, it may be advantageous to check out incorporation.

Note: the IRS understands if you lose money in the first couple of years in business, but **a sole proprietor or S**

corp should show a profit at least three out of five years. Otherwise the IRS may call your writing a "hobby" and your deductions will be limited or disallowed. This situation does not apply to C corporations.

RETIREMENT

Years ago, I started contributing to a retirement plan . . . and now that my husband is retired, I'm glad I did. The retirement plan helps us make ends meet now that we're both over sixty-five.

One way I keep my corporation from making a profit is by contributing as much as allowable to my retirement plan. Every time I write myself a paycheck, I make a personal contribution to the plan and my company makes an even larger contribution.

I suggest you speak to a financial advisor about the type of retirement program that's best for you. But first, read the section on retirement in Judith McQuown's book, *Inc Yourself.* It will give you the information you need to make an informed decision.

ACCOUNTING SYSTEM

One more thing to consider: when you first set up a business, you must establish whether you are operating on a **cash** or **accrual system**. Are you going to claim income *when you are paid* or *when you have actually completed the work?* Writers need to give this special attention, because we often receive partial payments for long-term work.

For instance: you sign a book contract, and within thirty days you receive an advance check for $1,000. You have not yet finished the book, but you put the money in the bank and start spending because you have bills. Your book won't be finished until next year, when you will hand it in and receive another check for $1,000 on delivery and acceptance.

If you are operating under the **cash system**, you count that first $1,000 as income on the day you receive the check. You will count the second check for $1,000 on the day you receive it next year. When you pay your taxes, you will count $1,000 as income in the first year, and $1,000 as income in the second year.

But if you are operating under the **accrual system**, you put the check in the bank and spend it, but you do not claim it as income until the *book is complete and accepted*. When you receive the second check for delivery and acceptance of your manuscript, you put it in the bank. When you pay your taxes, you will count *both checks as income* in the *second* year, because that's when the job was completed.

I have found the accrual system to be advantageous because I can offset larger income amounts with larger expenses. I would wait to buy an expensive new computer or take a research trip to Europe, for instance, in the second year, when I would have the larger amount counted as income. Using the accrual system is a smart way to balance expenses and income, especially if you sign a multi-book contract.

Whew. I don't know about you, but thinking about numbers and taxes and percentages makes my head spin. That's why I urge you to speak to your financial advisor before making any big decisions about business structure— once you're set up, it's not easy to go back and start over.

Chapter Eleven

COPYRIGHT

COPYRIGHT LAWS DIFFER FROM COUNTRY TO COUNTRY—I was amazed to discover that Great Britain has no copyright registration system. But the United States does, so let's discuss it.

A piece of creative work is copyrighted the moment you create it. It's your book or poem or song or painting. But it is not *registered* until you send a copy of that work to the U.S. Copyright office, pay a fee, and have it legally registered.

If you write a book, the manuscript is protected by copyright law from the moment you create it, But if you sell the publishing rights to a traditional publisher, they will register the copyright for you. If you self-publish, you should (but are not required to) register the copyright yourself. You'll need to fill out a form and send a copy of the work (paper or digital) to the copyright office. You can get started here: https://www.copyright.gov/registration/.

If you do an Internet search for "register copyright," you'll find dozens of sites who will charge you to fill out the same forms you'd have to fill out on the official copyright registration site. Avoid these companies. The official website listed above will walk you through the process.

Why do we register copyrights? Copyright establishes your authorship and registers the date of creation, thus protecting your work from others who would later claim to own the copyright and publishing rights.

The piracy of literary works occurs every day on the Internet. If you find your book on an unauthorized site, you can file a copyright claim and ask to have it removed. The procedure is simple, but when you find nearly all of your books online (as I have), the process can be labor intensive. People may think this sort of piracy is harmless, but it robs authors and other creators of the income they need to keep creating.

Don't support these piracy sites and report them when you can.

If someone steals your work and sells it as their own, your first recourse is to report the seller. On Amazon, for instance, tell Amazon support that someone is selling your book under their name. Do the same on any other sites. Filing a lawsuit is an expensive last resort, which is why few people sue for copyright infringement.

Don't forget about the Author's Guild legal department. If someone has stolen your work and none of your efforts to rectify the situation have been successful, you should join the Author's Guild and speak to their lawyers. Sometimes a letter from a lawyer is enough to convince book pirates to stop their piracy.

I should mention one other method of protecting your copyright. This concept has been around forever and I'm not sure it still works, but here it is:

Print a copy of your completed work and mail it to

yourself. When it arrives, make sure the postmark shows the date and file the envelope away *unopened*.

The dated, unopened envelope will demonstrate that you created the work before any would-be imitator. I'm not sure the idea would stand up in court, but there it is— the poor man's copyright protection.

Chapter Twelve

TRADITIONAL VERSUS INDEPENDENT PUBLISHING

SHOULD YOU WRITE A BOOK AND PUBLISH IT YOURSELF? I'm going to be brutally honest with you—indie publishing works in some situations, but it is not the best avenue for publishing. For most people, traditional publishing, in which an established company pays you for the right to publish your book, is still the best way to publish even though the royalty percentages are far greater in indie publishing.

Why would I say that? Because traditional publishers offer distribution, marketing, professional editing, and design all in one deal, plus they pay you instead of you having to pay to have your book published.

Getting a slot at a traditional publisher isn't easy—if it were, everyone would do it. You'll have to do your best work, you might have to have an agent to even get your manuscript through the door, and you might have to adapt your creative concept for your book to have the best chance at selling in bookstores. But traditional publishing still beats indie publishing in most situations.

Independent publishing does offer some advantages

over traditional publishing. First, if your book is so focused on a niche or small market that a traditional publisher wouldn't be interested, go indie.

If you need to put a book out quickly, go indie (though I once wrote a timely book for a traditional publisher that was edited, printed, and released in six weeks).

If you want complete control over your work, go indie.

If you want to be able to make corrections or additions in a heartbeat, go indie.

But do all of these advantages give self-publishing an edge over traditional? I don't think so.

I publish both traditionally and independently, and I can tell you that my traditionally published books sell thousands of copies while my indie books sell hundreds. Same author. Same quality of writing. But *distribution* makes the difference.

Bookstores typically don't want to carry independently published books, so your book will probably be available only at online bookstores. Being listed on Amazon is great, but being listed on Amazon along with millions of other titles means you book could well get lost in the crowd.

As an indie publisher, you will be responsible for marketing your book and selling it. If you have time to speak in front of groups to push your book, and if you have extra money to spend on social media ads and email promotions, go for it. But if you have neither the time nor money for marketing, your book is likely to languish.

A lawyer friend of mine published a book on Florida law and traveled around the state, meeting bookstore owners and convincing them to carry his book. He published it independently because a national publisher wouldn't be interested in a book that would sell in only one of the fifty states. For him, independent publishing was a wise choice.

Be aware of the so-called "vanity" or subsidy presses.

These companies will sell you a package, complete with editing, interior and cover design, printing, and x number of copies. They will promise that your book will be listed in their catalog, advertised online, and be available on Amazon and other online bookstore sites. They may offer postcards, bookmarks, and other promo materials for you to distribute. They may promise a marketing campaign, though that may simply consist of putting your book in their online catalog, which few people will see.

These packages are not inexpensive. Before you sign a contract with such a company, read the fine print, particularly the section about what is required if you want to cancel the contract and withdraw your title.

A young man who took my writing class heard me issue this warning, but he was eager to get his novel published, so he signed a deal with a subsidy press. His novel was the first book in a trilogy. When he became unhappy with the publisher's performance, he tried to get the rights to his first book reverted so he could take his trilogy elsewhere, but he couldn't.

Some subsidy publishers will point out—correctly—that it is less expensive to print books in large quantities, but do you have room to store one or two thousand books? How will you sell and ship them?

Most people today self-publish with Print On Demand (POD) publishers, which only publish books as they are ordered. Yes, it is more expensive to print one or two books at a time, but when you consider the cost of warehousing and distributing vast quantities of books, POD seems much more reasonable.

Before you rush to self-publish your work, consider this reality: it is easier to be traditionally published with *no* sales record than with a *poor* sales record, which you might have if you self-publish. You might think that a traditional publisher will somehow find your self-published book and want to pick it up and publish it at his house . . . hasn't that happened before. Yes—but that situation is unlikely unless your indie published book sells ten to twenty thousand copies.

Yet writers who study the craft, query publishers, and work hard to hone their writing are offered traditional book contracts every day.

MARSHMALLOWS

A researcher decided to study a group of four-year-olds. He offered them one marshmallow but said if they'd wait ten minutes while he stepped out of the room, they'd get two.

- 1/3 of the kids took the one marshmallow immediately.
- 1/3 took the one marshmallow after five minutes.
- 1/3 of the group waited ten minutes and got two marshmallows when the researcher returned.

He kept tabs on these kids all through school. Fourteen years later, the kids who had waited for two marshmallows were higher achievers and had SAT scores an average of 210 points higher than the others.[1]

My point? Don't rush to self-publish just because you can. Give yourself time to learn and polish your skills.

Double marshmallows are worth the wait.

---

1. Another account of the experiment is found here: https://www.simplypsychology.org/marshmallow-test.html, accessed April 20, 2024.

Chapter Thirteen

MARKETING

WHEN I STARTED WRITING, PUBLISHERS WERE responsible for doing all the marketing. They put print ads in magazines, attended big book conventions where they paid for their authors to attend and sign books, and hosted huge events for booksellers and bookstore owners.

Those days are gone. The big events have evolved into smaller trade shows and the conventions have become conferences that focus on educating retailers. Print ads are no longer the focus; most marketing money now goes to social media.

And though the responsibility for marketing still rests with the publisher, publishers expect authors to participate in marketing as well. Gone are the days when writers wrote and publishers marketed—now everyone works together to get the word out.

The rise of independent publishing can complicate the issue. Now the traditional publisher's books are featured alongside self-published books on Facebook and Instagram, and sometimes it's impossible to tell which is which. Competition is keener.

Everyone wants to know the best way to sell books, and no one has a certain answer. So many factors come into play—the genre of the book, the cover design, the marketing budget, and the book's competition at the time of release—not to mention the author's reputation, platform, social media profile, and personality.

SOCIAL MEDIA

Some people are natural born influencers—they're photogenic, they have wonderful voices, they don't stammer in videos, and they could sell mosquitos to Floridians. Others write good books, but they don't feel comfortable in front of a camera.

Here's the golden rule: *do what is right for you but do something.*

Years ago, I gathered names and addresses for a mailing list. I sent out a paper newsletter, two pages, printed front and back and stapled together. Postage was cheap in those days but mailing to my small list cost a healthy chunk of change—not to mention hours of work.

After a while, I stopped sending newsletters and started sending postcards featuring new releases. The postage was less expense, and I could design, print, and mail the postcards myself. Still expensive.

Then the world went digital, thank goodness. Today, like most authors, I have a reader's mailing list and send out a quarterly email newsletter about new releases, chatty news, and information about book discounts, if I know of any. My newsletter isn't about gaining new readers, it's about nurturing the current ones.

I once took an expensive course on Facebook advertising. The guru advised sending out a weekly newsletter, using Facebook ads, and hard-selling. I tried sending a weekly newsletters and found that my readers didn't appreciate receiving multiple emails—they unsubscribed. For books—which come out every few months, not every week—I didn't see how weekly emails could be effective. I went back to my old system of quarterly newsletters.

I have writer friends, however, who send out frequent emails and have devised winning formulas. They talk about their lives and their work, and they do so in such charming ways that their readers love getting their newsletters. That format works for them, but I don't have the energy to write my books *and* charming weekly emails. Apparently my charm has a limit.

What I *do* have time for is interaction on Facebook. I have found that daily interaction helps keep my readers connected, and I don't always talk about books. I write about my chickens, I post pictures of my dogs, and I expound on the adventures of life in woodsy Florida. Sometimes I ask for readers' opinions on a scene and I honestly value and listen to the responses. I find beta readers (test readers) through my Facebook page. Sometimes I hold giveaways on my page and award books or something I've made.

Instagram? I have an account, but the interaction there isn't as strong as on Facebook. Twitter? Not for me. TikTok? Ditto. But I have friends who love TikTok and Instagram and have hundreds of followers on each. If a platform works for you, have at it!

I recently started a channel on substack, but it's for writers who are seriously seeking a career in words.[1] Not a reader's channel at all.

When it comes to social media, find your niche and settle in it. Do what comes naturally to you, and your

---

1. Newsletter for writers: angelahunt.substack.com

readers will find you. Just be sure you're not spending more time on marketing than on writing.

OFFERING FREEBIES AND BARGAINS

Independent authors can easily boost their sales by offering free or low-priced books. If you publish your book through Amazon's KDP program and enroll your title in Kindle Unlimited, once every quarter you are allowed to offer your book free for five days. You select the five days, then you get the word out. How do you do that?

Probably the best way is through BookBub (www.BookBub.com). Book Bub users sign up for emails in their favorite genres, then every day they receive an email about free and bargain books in their genres. But BookBub is such a popular program that it's a challenge to get your title chosen for a BookBub offer. They examine the cover, the number of reviews, and the reviewers' star rating, then choose only the books that are likely to be popular with their readers.

Bookbub's service is not cheap—depending on the genre of your book (the more popular the genre, the higher the fee), it can cost over $1,000 to get your book offered as a BookBub deal. But here's the best news—every time I've done a BookBub deal, I've earned back every penny and then some. Best of all, those books continued to sell long after the deal expired.

BookBub also offers ads, so if your title wasn't chosen for a BookBub deal, you can place a BookBub ad. They offer blog articles that will teach you how to create an effective ad. So sign up for the BookBub mailing list and learn how to use this tool.

A less expensive option for book marketing is bookmarketingtools.com. After you've scheduled your Amazon

KDP title for five free days, use their submission tool to send the news of your free book to newsletters that alert readers to book bargains.

One caveat: I have noticed that some writers offer free books so frequently that they train their readers to expect freebies. Why should they buy, when sooner or later that title will be offered for nothing? So while offering free books to *influencers and book reviewers* is always a good idea, I suspect that offering books to *readers* for a low price—say, 99 cents for a limited period—is a better one. Just my opinion.

KDP offers a "countdown deal" as an alternative to the five days of free. In a countdown deal, the book is offered at 99 cents the first day of the deal and increases slightly every day thereafter, encouraging readers to buy early. Just make sure you readers are alerted to the lowest price *before* the countdown begins.

OTHER MARKETING OPPORTUNITIES

Your local communities may offer other opportunities for you to sell books. Depending on your title's subject, you could offer to speak at churches, service clubs like Rotary or Kiwanis, or other community events. Talk about the subject of your book and sell copies afterward.

Some libraries and colleges hold book fairs and literary festivals where you could set up a booth and spend a lovely morning selling your books and talking about your work. Check with your local library to see if you could give a talk about your topic and sell books afterward. Ask if they have a writers' group who might be interested in hearing about your publishing experience.

If you do an Internet search for "book marketing," you'll find all kinds of groups who will, for a fee, market your book. My publisher has engaged groups that do professional "blog tours," and those seem to work well.

What's a blog tour? The group finds readers who love to read, gives them a free digital copy of the book, and asks them to post a blog and a review (on sites like Goodread s.com) during a predetermined week. The bloggers are not required to write positive reviews. But during that week, several people review your book and the miracle of "word of mouth" begins. If the reviews are positive, others will read the reviews and order your book . . . at least, that's the result we want.

Blog tours are especially useful if the reviews post on Amazon during or just after the book's release. (Amazon does not allow reviews to be posted until the book's official release date.) But if Amazon staffers think you've asked friends and family to bombard the site with five-star reviews, Amazon will remove them. The reviews that work best on Amazon are from the "verified purchasers."

If you hire a group to help promote your book, be careful. Try to find one of their former clients who can vouch for their effectiveness.

The Independent Book Publishers of America[2] (IBPA) offers a service to its members that might be helpful in your marketing plan. For instance, Netgalley.com is a site for professional book reviewers and librarians. For a reduced fee, IBPA members can upload their titles to the site, where reviewers and librarians can download the book, read it, and leave a review. These reviewers will also be honest, so make sure your book is ready to be evaluated by the pros before you publish it.

You can also work with other writers to market each other's books. A brilliant writer friend of mine organizes a

---

2. https://www.ibpa-online.org/

readers' scavenger hunt twice a year. She finds about twenty authors with releases near the time of the hunt, then she organizes a reader's hunt for clues with great prizes.

Other writers come together to link their blogs, promote each other's books, and have giveaways. Use your imagination—there is power in numbers!

WHAT DOESN'T WORK

I've made many attempts to market books over the years, and I can tell you a few things that don't work well:

1. Bling. Pens inscribed with the author's name, mugs with a book title, flashlights with a website engraved on the side—they don't sell books. They do make curious knickknacks.

2. Selling indie-published books at retail out of my garage—why should people order a book directly from me when they can order from Amazon and get overnight delivery? Yet one garage sale *did* work—in the months before we moved, I offered five books for ten bucks and even threw in some foreign language editions—I told the recipients to take them to their local libraries, which often need books for their foreign language collections. I made some cash (though not much profit) and moved a ton of books!

Note: if you have published traditionally, selling books out of your garage will likely violate your contract. Bookstores have enough competition; they shouldn't have to worry about competing with your garage sales.

3. Fancy editions: I once offered some children's books with customized dedication pages, printed specially at the publisher—I sold two copies.

4. Autographed books: having an author's signature on a book is fun, but it doesn't carry the cachet it used to.

5. Speaking at schools: while I love speaking to children,

I found that all the schools wanted me to speak gratis and children don't have money to buy books. Speaking to kids is fun, but all that speaking cut into my writing, so I had to stop. Now I try to do the Great American Teach-In every year, so I can speak to kids *and* stick to my schedule.

As I write this, I've just come from a retreat where several multi-published writers talked about the marketing techniques they've used: Facebook ads. Amazon ads. Bookbub deals. They all work to some extent, but they all involve an investment of money and time. You're likely to find YouTube videos on how to use these and similar programs, so check them out, set your budget carefully, and learn all you can before venturing into the marketing waters.

Chapter Fourteen

EQUIPPING YOUR OFFICE

A WRITER CAN GET BY WITH SURPRISINGLY LITTLE. Something to write *on* and something to write *with* are really all you need to get started, but operating a business requires a little more.

What will you need in order to set up your company? You could begin with a pencil and tablet, but an editor will expect you to submit a manuscript that has been properly typed and formatted (double spaced, 1-inch margins on all sides except the top, which should be 1.5 inches, black ink, font Times New Roman size 12). Realistically, you will need a computer with Internet capability, a word processing program, and a printer. Most documents are formatted in Microsoft Word, though many writers use Scrivener as their writing program.

SOFTWARE

Scrivener is not AI—it is not going to write for you. It's a word processor designed for writers, a program that allows you to write novels, screenplays, or nonfiction in the proper format. I have used Scrivener to write novels, nonfiction, and my dissertation. It offers a spell checker, a read-aloud function, and it automatically backs up your document so you never have to worry that a power outage will cause you to lose your work.

Scrivener offers several ways to export your manuscript, even as a Kindle file or a Word document. Quite simply, it has every writing feature Word offers, but none of the features that writers never use.

I wrote dozens of books without Scrivener, so it's not a requirement, but it's so useful that now I can't imagine writing without it. With Scrivener open, you'll have a place to write, a place to save and quickly refer to your research notes, and a way to see all your material at a glance. If you write in sections, Scrivener will allow you to see each section, so you won't have to scroll through an entire document to find the spot you want to edit. Scrivener is reasonably priced, too, and it is not a subscription, so you won't have to make annual payments. Best of all, there's a thirty-day free trial so you can experiment with it. Many people teach online classes in how to use Scrivener, but if you're familiar with Word, you probably won't need the classes. There are plenty of YouTube videos available to answer any questions you may have while working with Scrivener. You can download your free trial at literatureandlatte.com.

BUT—as wonderful as Scrivener is, most editors want to receive a document formatted in Word. You can export your Scrivener document as a Word file, but you should review it to make sure it is formatted correctly, so you will either need Word or access to a Word-compatible program.

You will also need some sort of software to handle your accounting. Quicken has a suite of products, everything from simple Quicken to Quickenbooks, which includes features that allow you to run payroll. What you choose will depend on how you have set up your business.

In my early days, I experimented with software that was supposed to help me plot books, but I never found them useful. I have also experimented with AI programs that help you analyze your manuscript, and I have found Autocrat useful. I don't use it for plotting or in early drafts, but it functions as another pair of editorial "eyes" in the polishing stage. But it's not necessary. If you are using other AI programs that check grammar, etc., just be aware that they can polish fiction to a point where it becomes unnatural. Fictional characters rarely use perfect grammar, so don't rely too heavily on grammar and language programs.

FURNISHINGS

What else will you need to set up your business?

Your office will need a desk and a chair (hopefully, a comfortable one, since you will be spending hours in it), and adequate lighting. You will also need blank paper and a notebook or notepad for scribbled thoughts and reminders. A calendar is also useful, whether paper or digital, because part of being a professional writer is remembering to meet your deadlines.

As a writer, you will undoubtedly collect books. Reference books, novels, nonfiction books, and books about the writing craft. You can borrow them from the library, of course, but if they are useful, you may want to keep them and make notes in the margin. I have hundreds of books, and though I purge them every time we move, I have kept some for years . . . because one day I might need them again.

You will also need a filing cabinet, a notebook for published clips, another notebook for corporation documents, and files for contracts, notes, and correspondence. Your accountant will expect you to keep tax records and receipts for income and expenses for at least seven years, and you will want to keep notes on the articles and books you've written. You will also want to keep a folder for each book—keep the contract, editorial notes, copies of good reviews, and any title-related correspondence in that folder. If you're writing for magazines, keep a tear sheet of each printed article. You never know when you'll want to go back and look up some detail in that piece.

What you do *not* need to keep are drafts of your books. While they may have sentimental value, the place to store your finished projects is on a properly backed up computer disk, not in your office. My office would be a fire hazard and roach heaven if I had paper drafts of each of my books stacked against the walls.

Instead I save the final versions on a computer file, which is backed up to *two* external hard drives every 12 hours. Yes, I'm over cautious, but as of this writing, I've never lost a file.

Find a space or spare room in your home and make it your writing area. Clear out the distractions and bring in your desk, chair, and computer. In time, you'll realize what else you need, and adapt the space to suit.

I have writer friends who can't work without background music; others can't write unless the room is silent. Some writers like a window; others find a window distracting.

Do what works best for you.

SHOULD YOU HIRE A VIRTUAL ASSISTANT?

The first time I heard the term *virtual assistant*, I envisioned an AI computer program that would speak in

Alexa's voice and answer my phone calls. But a virtual assistant is actually human, a remote secretary. A VA can monitor your social media accounts, post memes that promote your book, handle routine correspondence, and book your travel reservations. They can update your website, check for new book reviews, and moderate your Facebook readers group. They can do whatever you need them to do.

How much will you pay a virtual assistant? Since these individuals work remotely, they usually have more than one client, so you don't have to support a full-time employee. They are independent contractors, so you won't have to put them on the payroll or pay their health benefits. You will pay them for hours worked. The national average salary for a VA is $25, but the hourly wage ranges from $7.25 to $37.50.

To find a VA, do an Internet search for "hire a virtual assistant" and you'll find scores of them, many with reviews and a list of their skills. You'll probably want someone with strong computer and clerical skills (a writer shouldn't have posts with misspelled words!) and a knack for organization. You might want to hire someone for a couple of weeks and see how well the arrangement works.

I've never hired a virtual assistant, so I can't speak to the benefits of having one, and but I have writer friends who depend on their VAs. A virtual assistant may be a life-saver for you and a worthwhile investment.

Chapter Fifteen

WRITER'S CONFERENCES

I ATTENDED MY FIRST WRITER'S CONFERENCE AFTER I'D started writing books. I sat in on several unique classes—one on screenwriting piqued my curiosity, though I didn't see myself ever actually writing a screenplay. Sometimes it's smart to study other forms of writing just to increase your knowledge base.

I learned then that most writer's conferences are geared to those who are getting started in the business. That doesn't mean they're not useful—indeed, you can learn in one three-day conference what it took me five years to learn on my own. Conferences offer a lot of information in a short period, and it's difficult to absorb everything.

Many conferences offer recordings of their classes—I recommend that you order the recordings that appeal to you and listen to them throughout the year, absorbing what you need when you need it. Much easier to do than trying to guzzle an entire fountain of knowledge in one three-day weekend.

Writer's conferences are wonderful for networking, especially those that have gatherings for people from the same geographical areas. You might find a critique group or partner who will be able to help you—and vice versa—throughout the year. You may establish what will prove to be a lifelong friendship at a conference.

Many conferences offer attendees the opportunity to sit down and meet with editors and agents—and face-to-face meetings can be important. Go prepared to those meetings with a proposal in hand, but don't try to describe your entire novel in one breath. Give a brief synopsis, be pleasant, and offer to leave the proposal and your business card if the editor or agent expresses an interest. Most of them, however, will probably give you *their* card, and ask you to send something once you've returned home. When you get home, send the material, and remind the editor or agent that they asked to hear from you.

It's also fine to sit with an agent or editor and chat—to ask, for instance, what they are looking for in the months ahead. If you have a question about publishing, this is the perfect time to find an answer.

Sometimes you can meet with published authors as well. While authors don't have the ability to purchase or publish a manuscript, they can usually read the first page or two and give input about the writing and/or story formation, especially if the writer provides a brief synopsis.

So if a conference offers these one-on-one opportunities (they are usually fifteen-minute appointments), be sure to take advantage of them. Other conferences will allow you to submit a partial manuscript for critique by an editor, author, or agent, sometimes for a fee.

When you are at the conference, dress professionally and be prepared to make a pleasant first impression—because that opportunity will never come again. You may find yourself seated with other authors, agents, and editors at mealtimes, so feel free to ask questions of anyone who is willing to talk. But if an editor or agent seems exhausted or quiet—let them rest. Writers' conferences can be exhausting.

You may have heard the apocryphal story about an editor who was followed into the ladies' room by a woman who shoved her proposal under the door of the bathroom stall. I don't know if the story is true but trust me—don't be that woman.

Most writer's conferences also offer on-site bookstores that sell copies of the presenting authors' titles and many fine books on the craft of writing, sometimes at a discount. This is a perfect time to collect great material, so leave room in your suitcase!

Conferences, of course, usually reflect the character of the hosting organization. The conference held by American Christian Fiction Writers features times of worship and prayer. Conferences sponsored by mystery writers may offer classes on police work and forensics. Many will have a well-known author as a keynote speaker. Some conferences are small and intimate, some are huge, with banquets, awards ceremonies to honor contest winners, and late-night events.

You may want to consider attending a writer's workshop. Workshops are usually smaller than conferences, and while they do feature instruction, they also give a participant time to incorporate the lessons learned from the instruction. Writer's workshops typically involve learning-by-doing and can be very beneficial.

You can go back to your room and write at a writer's conference, of course—*if* you have the energy. With so many speakers packed into each day, few folks do.

Chapter Sixteen

WHEN CAN YOU QUIT YOUR DAY JOB?

So you want to be a professional writer . . . but the thought of losing your job security scares you spitless. How can you know you're doing the right thing?

If you have a spouse who can support you during the early days, count yourself fortunate. My husband had a full-time job and health insurance, which allowed me to quit my day job and start writing full time. After a year, I was earning as much by writing as I had been making at my full-time job.

If you are employed part-time, you may want to keep your job while you get started. Working a job *and* writing requires self-discipline—you have to write during your writing time and fend off the urge to procrastinate. Though you have no boss standing over you, you'll have to put in the hours if you want to earn the income you need.

When your writing income equals or surpasses your *other* income, you can safely quit the first job.

You may find that the family budget is best supported by part-time day job and part-time writing. I have several novelist friends who work jobs they love and write in the evenings or on weekends. It may take longer to accomplish your goals if you're working another job, but that's okay. If you write and polish only a page per day, you can easily write a book a year.

Freelancing gives you wonderful flexibility—you can work on Sundays and relax on Tuesdays, and you can write in your pajamas if you like—but if you want to get paid, you have to sell articles and/or books. You have to keep projects circulating among editors, and you have to mind your calendar and block out dates for individual projects.

When I sign a contract for a novel, I know I'm going to need to reserve about five months for that book. I usually work five days a week, which means I spent about a month on each of my five drafts. So I literally print out a calendar, mark through dates for which I have other commitments, and then give myself an assignment for every available day. During the first draft, I have to write so many words per day—they don't have to be *perfect* words, but I have to put words into the computer.

In subsequent drafts, I'm not counting words, but editing pages, so I assign myself a certain number of pages to edit per day. Every morning I sit down and work on my daily quota—and when I've reached the number of words or pages, I'm done. I leave the office and live my life.

We all have days when things don't go according to plan, so when that happens, simply adjust your calendar. As long as you're finished by your deadline, you'll be fine. It helps to have a certain number of unassigned days on the calendar for things like illness and family emergencies. If you finish *before* your deadline, celebrate!

Friends and neighbors may assume that because you're working from home, you're free to drop everything to have lunch or take the day off on a whim. You'll have to remind them that you're still working. Covid made working from home more commonplace, but some folks will still assume that life as a freelance writer is a life of leisure.

I would encourage you to find time for friendship with fellow writers—no one understands a writer's challenges like one who's walked the same path. Writers' organizations abound online, so find one that suits you and participate in their email lists and conferences. You'll be thrilled to meet people who share your passion for writing.

A final word: the writing life is not for everyone. A successful writer must be self-motivated, disciplined, and able to spend long hours toiling alone. A writer must be flexible and have a relatively thick skin, because no one is going to enjoy *everything* you write.

But if you persevere, and if you're willing to learn, you can sell your writing at hundreds of outlets. People will read your words, and you just might change a few hearts and minds for good.

I once painted these words on my office wall: *The act of writing is the act of discovering what you believe.* That's true, because writing about life forces you to test your own beliefs and principles. Whether you write fiction or nonfiction, writing is opening your inner self and sharing it with someone else . . . in the hope that you will affect them in some way.

For the better, I hope. Otherwise, why do it?

WRITER'S ASSOCIATIONS

Writer's Associations

If you want to find a local writing or critique group, start at your local library. Your librarian may know of a group that meets in the library, so be sure to check there first.

Many of the groups listed below have membership requirements and annual dues or a membership fee. Many have annual conferences, where writers meet for education, friendship, and to learn about development in the industry. Visit their websites to learn more and see if one could benefit you.

Authors' Guild: https://authorsguild.org. The largest organization for professional writers in America. Works for the benefit of authors in political and cultural fields, keeping tabs on issues such as AI, copyright infringement, and other legal issues that affect authors. Has a legal department available to aid members.

American Christian Fiction Writers (ACFW). http://acfw.com For published and unpublished fiction writers who are Christians. Features a blog, an email list, a national conference, and contests.

Cat Writers Association: https://catwriters.com. Yes, an association of people who write about cats.

Dog Writers Association of America: https://dogwriters.org. Since 1935, the organization dedicated to writing about man's best friend.

Historical Novel Society: https://historicalnovelsoci ety.org. For readers and writers of historical fiction.

Independent Book Publishers Association: https://www.ibpa-online.org. If you plan to publish independently, IBPA can give you several benefits: education, programs, and discounts on publishing services. Definitely worth checking out.

Mystery Writers of America: http://mysterywriter s.org. For readers and writers of mysteries.

National Association of Independent Writers and Editors: https://naiwe.com. This is a professional organization for freelance writers and editors, both commercial and literary. They provide professional support and career development for members through their many benefits, including an individual NAIWE website for each member, plus access to virtual training and career-development events and inclusion in a searchable database.

National Association of Memoir Writers: https://www.namw.org. For writers who are writing their life stories.

Novelists Inc. https://ninc.com/about/. An organization for multi-published novelists. Has an email list and a national conference.

Romance Writers of America: http://rwa.org. Promotes writing and writers of romance, the most popular genre. Has an email list, the RITA award contest, and a national conference.

Science Fiction and Fantasy Writers Association: https://www.sfwa.org. Founded in 1965, SFWA is for published authors and industry professionals in the fields of science fiction, fantasy, and related genres. Has contests, a national conference, and email lists.

Sisters in Crime: https://www.sistersincrime.org. An organization to promote female mystery writers.

Society of Children's Book Writers and Illustrators: https://www.scbwi.org. For those who specialize in writing and/or illustrating for children.

Western Writers of America: https://westernwriters.org. Not for writers who live in the west, but for writers who write *of* the American west.

Women's Fiction Writers Association: https://www.womensfictionwriters.org. Not for women who write fiction, but for people who write women's fiction. Women's fiction is not romance, but centers on the emotional journey of women.

Word Weavers International: https://word-weavers.com. Founded in 1997, Word Weavers International is dedicated to providing a forum for Christian writers to critique one another's work in a face-to-face format, whether in a traditional chapter or in Word Weavers' unique online "pages," to improve craft. Writers of all levels are welcome.

EXERCISES

1. TAKE SOME TIME TO WRITE OUT YOUR REASONS FOR wanting a career as a professional writer. Do you have an overall goal? Can you see yourself writing for years to come? Do you think you can support yourself and/or your family through a writing career?

2. How do you respond to criticism? Most editors suggest changes in order to improve a book—can you put yourself in the editor's position and see his or her point? How will you handle bad reviews? Not everyone will be your ideal reader, so how will you feel when you read a less than glowing review? Can you shrug it off?

3. Would you be more comfortable working for yourself (with all those attendant responsibilities) or writing for a company or magazine? Which would be more suitable for your family? Write out a list of pros and cons for each possibility: entrepreneur or employee. Which would be better for you?

4. Before you read this book, how much did you think the average American writer earned? To earn enough to

support a family, you'll have to either write as an employee or sell a *lot* of books and/or articles. Does that idea appeal to you, or do you find it daunting?

NOTES

www.ingramcontent.com/pod-product-compliance
Lightning Source LLC
Chambersburg PA
CBHW070027030426
42335CB00017B/2321